IMAGES
of America

FORT BENNING

IMAGES
of America

FORT BENNING

Kenneth H. Thomas Jr.

ARCADIA

First published 2003
Reprinted 2003

Published by Arcadia Publishing
Charleston SC, Chicago IL, Portsmouth NH, San Francisco CA

Printed in the United States of America

Library of Congress Catalog Card Number: 2003107595

For all general information contact Arcadia Publishing at:
Telephone 843-853-2070
Fax 843-853-0044
E-mail sales@arcadiapublishing.com
For customer service and orders:
Toll-Free 1-888-313-2665

Visit us on the internet at http://www.arcadiapublishing.com

CONTENTS

ACKNOWLEDGMENTS

My most loyal and enthusiastic supporter for this book has been my mother, Louise Brooks Thomas, whose assistance I greatly appreciate. My sister Melissa and her husband Jim Thomas also lent their encouragement for this effort. Katie White, Southeast Publisher for Arcadia Publishing, lent enthusiastic support early on for me to pursue this topic.

The book could not have been accomplished without access to the photograph collection at the National Infantry Museum at Fort Benning. I greatly appreciate the help and enthusiasm of Z. Frank Hanner, director; Jill Kiah-Saslav, contract consultant; Lt. Col. (Ret.) Bob Felton, the volunteer who organized and oversees the photograph collection; and Becky Pennington, secretary. They made my several visits to the museum a pleasurable experience. I also appreciate the early interest in this book of Maj. Gen. (Ret.) Jerry White, former Infantry School Commandant, now Chairman of the Board of the National Infantry Foundation and Ben Williams, Executive Director of the National Infantry Foundation.

I could not have completed this book, which required a great deal of computer scanning, without the valuable scanning and technical assistance of James R. Lockhart and Carolyn B. Kidd. I also appreciate the photographic duplication help of Stephen F. Schwab of Jack's Camera Shop.

Many people, both connected with their institutions or as individuals, provided valuable research assistance and advice as well as, in some cases, loaned material for this book. They are as follows: Linda Aaron (University of Georgia, Hargrett Library); Margaret Calhoon (Georgia Power Company); Ed Callahan (member, OCS Alumni Association); Curt Teich Postcard Company Archives in Lake County, Illinois; the DeKalb County Public Library staff, especially Barbara Kelly and Graham Reiney; Gail Miller Deloach (Georgia Division of Archives and History); Sarah O. Dunaway and Jane Durden; Dan Elliott; G. Richard Elwell; Lewis P. Fern; the Georgia Postcard Club; Reagan Grimsley (Columbus State University Archives); Jean Overby Harron; Col. (Ret.) James Hayes; the Historic Preservation Division of the Georgia Department of Natural Resources staff, where I work, especially Serena Bellew, Richard Cloues, and W. Ray Luce; Edward Howard; Linda Kennedy (Historic Linwood Foundation); Kaye L. Minchew (Troup County Archives); Michael Nagy (Salvation Army Archives); Polly Nodine (Jimmy Carter Presidential Library); Doug Purcell (Historic Chattahoochee Commission); Peter Roberts (Georgia State University Special Collections); and Charles L. Skipworth, former co-owner of the Columbus Photo Service.

Besides the above, other individuals offered me material from their private collections for use in the book, much of which was included. They are: Mary Frances Ahern, Carl Anderson, Alek Ansley, Bob Basford, David Brady (the Columbus Armory), Beth Grashof, Jane Grider, Sally B. Hatcher, Mike Helms, Lucile Mehaffey Rushin Hunter, Alan J. Koman, John Mallory Land, Gayle Daley Nix, Deborah Long Palmer, Carl L. Patrick Sr., Mary Lewis Pierson, Evelyn Rushin Posey, Frank Schnell, John M. Sheftall, Christal Oliver Speer, and Susan Woodall-Stuckey.

I also could not have accomplished this project without the existence of eBay, Inc., the Internet's on-line auction site, through which I purchased some of the material used for this book.

Photo Credit Addendum: A majority of the photographs used herein were originally made by the United States Army and, except in a few cases, no attempt has been made to specify which unit, such as the Signal Corps, actually made the original photograph, as many are unmarked or came from publications. The Georgia Division of Archives and History is part of the office of the Secretary of State.

INTRODUCTION

On October 5, 1918, the arrival of members of the United States Army's Infantry School of Arms at the Union Depot in Columbus, Georgia, began a new era for both the infantry and for the city of Columbus. The city had just celebrated its 90th birthday, having been created in 1828 on Georgia's western frontier along the Chattahoochee River. The Infantry School of Arms was moving from Fort Sill, Oklahoma, to Camp Benning, the name proposed by several local organizations to honor Confederate Gen. Henry L. Benning, who had lived in Columbus. The name was made official on October 18th. The United States Army had been looking for a new, more adequate location for the school, one with better weather and terrain. Once the "powers that be" in Columbus learned that the city and its environs were under consideration, an intense lobbying campaign began as early as 1917 to have the school relocated to the Columbus area.

When the first soldiers arrived in Columbus at the railroad station on 6th Avenue (now the chamber of commerce), they marched two and one-half miles from there to the newly created encampment on Macon Road, which most recently was the 85-acre dairy farm of Alex Reid. The location was just at the eastern edge of the suburb of Wynnton, not yet within the Columbus city limits. While the troops settled into the temporary encampment on Macon Road, negotiations were already underway for the purchase of land for a permanent military post some nine miles from the city in the southern portion of Muscogee County and the northern portion of Chattahoochee County. The *Enquirer-Sun* announced on November 12, 1918, that proceedings would begin shortly in United States District Court to condemn thousands of acres of farmland and purchase it for the United States Army. The land owners were mostly small farmers with some larger land owners. One of these, Arthur Bussey of Columbus, owned a 1,750-acre plantation and dairy farm with a main house known as "Riverside," which would become the central part of the Main Post area. In June 1919, Camp Benning was moved from Macon Road, to the present Main Post area in Chattahoochee County, centered on the Bussey Plantation, with "Riverside" becoming the home of the Infantry School's commandant. On February 8, 1922, Camp Benning was elevated and became Fort Benning, as it remains today. While the first land acquisition brought the post to 97,000 acres, in 1941 a second acquisition of 65,000 additional acres in both Georgia and Alabama was begun and brought the size of the post to 162,000 acres. The official size today is 182,000 acres.

My interest in Fort Benning began in the early 1960s, when my grandparents, Joe and Helen Brooks, began to take me to the area of the "reservation" along Buena Vista Road where my grandfather's grandparents and other kin once lived. They had been among those small farmers whose land had been acquired by the Army for the military post. We would often visit the old cemeteries and my grandfather would point out the former home sites of his grandparents and others. These trips nurtured my beginning interest in genealogy and local history and it has been my good fortune for it to become my professional career.

As the 85th anniversary of the founding of Camp Benning began to get closer, I felt there was a need for a pictorial history of Fort Benning, as there was no book about the post that was currently available in the book market. Having already worked with Arcadia Publishing on a previous book, *Columbus, Georgia, in Vintage Postcards* (2001), I turned to them for this new venture. In seeking photographs and other illustrations for this book, I made use of my own postcard collection, several 1940s-era photo booklets about Fort Benning, and acquired many items on eBay, Inc., the Internet auction site. I also borrowed materials from several people acknowledged earlier. I felt that a general canvas of people in the Columbus area, heavy with retired military personnel, would probably have yielded too many items to evaluate for inclusion. I went instead to one of the largest sources of photographs of Fort Benning, the collection at the National Infantry Museum, which is located on the post. There, in the photographic archives, lies an estimated 100,000 photos. I was able to review only a small percentage of those, but hopefully have selected some important images for this book.

Due to the vast amount of material available and the publisher's limit on the number of illustrations that could be included, choices had to be made. I hope the selections will interest anyone with a connection to Fort Benning, whether they served there or their parent did. I have tried to tell a story through the captions, tacking down many items of interest and trivia about the post. There was no way to cover all aspects of its history; there are other books recently published or currently in the works by other authors who will hopefully do that. I have also chosen to conclude with 1978, using illustrations only up to then to give the book a more historical perspective.

So as we mark the 85th anniversary of Fort Benning's founding and the 175th anniversary of the founding of Columbus in 2003, we can reflect back on what the post and the Infantry School have meant to the Army, the community, and the nation. Many of those who served there have become national leaders. So many people who have come to and through Fort Benning have returned for other tours of duty. Many have married local residents and remained in the Columbus area as active members of the community. Others have returned there to retire as reflected by the fact that many of the current leaders of Columbus are retired military.

This book has not been officially "authorized," so the 220 illustrations and the text are my choices alone. I hope the book, which includes one of the largest collections of Fort Benning illustrations heretofore published, will serve as a reference source for anyone interested in the post's history. This look at the first 60 years of Fort Benning should bring back many memories for those who have served there and inspire those interested in preserving the history of this important military institution.

Kenneth H. Thomas, Jr.
June 26, 2003
Decatur, Georgia

One
CAMP BENNING
1918–1919

CAMP BENNING. After months of negotiating, the announcement was made in late August 1918 that the United States Army's Infantry School of Arms would be relocated from Fort Sill, Oklahoma, to Columbus, Georgia. *The Columbus Enquirer-Sun* announced on October 1 "Temporary Camp Ready For Soldiers" and that locals had helped to hurriedly build a military post on Macon Road, just past the Wynnton area. This photo was taken January 1919. (Courtesy of the National Infantry Museum.)

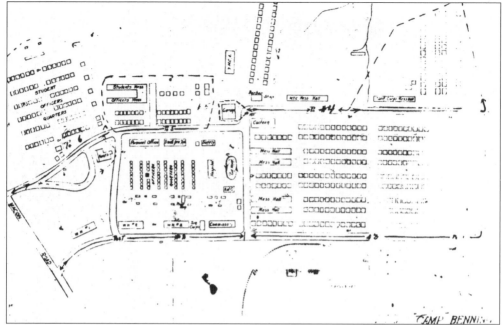

CAMP BENNING MAP. The camp was on Macon Road at what is now Dixon Drive. The 85-acre site was the dairy and cotton farm of Alexander Reid. Reid, the Irish-born husband of Grace Burrus, also managed the Rankin House, and later the Racine Hotel, and died in 1922. This March 1919 map shows numerous groupings of tents, for enlisted men and officers, and wooden support buildings. (Courtesy of the National Infantry Museum.)

CAMP BENNING, DETAIL OF TENTS. The first 367 soldiers arrived from Fort Sill on Sunday, October 5, 1918, and marched from the Union Depot in Columbus to the new site. The camp was officially begun the next day. This often seen photo, by Dixie Photo Company, shows a close-up of some of the 16-by-16 foot tents and wooden support buildings. (Courtesy of the Georgia Division of Archives and History and the National Infantry Museum.)

CAMP BENNING ACTIVITIES. In this 1918 view, soldiers are playing volleyball in a detachment street. The newspaper reported in November that the soldiers were "all fascinated by" volleyball. This layout of tents was very similar if not the same as you would find on any United States Army post where tents were used. The officers and enlisted men lived in separate tent groupings. (Courtesy of the National Infantry Museum.)

A SOLDIER AND HIS TENT. This unidentified soldier has his tent flap up, showing the cement base which the citizens of Columbus had helped construct. On the men's arrival, the newspaper reported that a "splendid looking body of men" were "highly pleased at [the] cordial reception given to them," a welcoming that would echo in Columbus for generations. The photo was taken by Wynnton resident Miss Josephine Banks Dimon. (Courtesy of John McKay Sheftall.)

11

SOLDIER WITH GAS MASK. This unidentified soldier was presumably modeling his gas mask for the ladies, in this case Wynnton resident Miss Josephine Banks Dimon, who lived a few blocks away at the Cedars, her family home. This view also shows his tent folded up. While the original Camp Benning site was always temporary, its close proximity to Wynnton is often forgotten. (Courtesy of John McKay Sheftall.)

RED CROSS VOLUNTEERS. These three young Columbus women are shown in their American Red Cross uniforms beside the Red Cross truck presumably at the city hospital. Miss Josephine Banks Dimon (later Mrs. John J. McKay Jr. of Macon), from whose album this and the preceding two photos were taken, is at the far right. The other ladies are unidentified. They were volunteering with the local chapter of the American Red Cross with the troops at Camp Benning. (Courtesy of John McKay Sheftall.)

PORTRAIT OF GEN. HENRY L. BENNING. The portrait of General Benning, the base's namesake, was unveiled at the Infantry School on June 6, 1940. Pictured are (from left to right) Miss Kate Edwards, the artist; Henry Benning Crawford, a grandson; Miss Augusta Benning Burgard, Crawford's granddaughter, who unveiled the portrait; and Brig. Gen. Asa Singleton, Infantry School commandant. The painting is now at the National Infantry Museum. (Courtesy of the National Infantry Museum.)

GENERAL BENNING'S GRAVESITE. A military ceremony and wreath laying takes place at General Benning's grave at Linwood Cemetery in Columbus to honor the base's namesake on October 6, 1968, the 50th anniversary of the founding of Camp Benning. In the foreground is the grave of the general's daughter, Miss Anna Caroline Benning (1853–1935), who had raised the flag at Camp Benning on December 12, 1918, at a large ceremony. (Courtesy of the National Infantry Museum.)

75TH ANNIVERSARY MARKER. The Diamond Jubilee, or 75th anniversary, of the founding of Camp Benning, was recognized in 1993 with the placement of a historical marker by the Historic Chattahoochee Commission with support from the Carl Patrick Foundation. The marker is located just off Wynnton Road/Macon Road on the north side at Dixon Drive and 15th Street in Columbus. (Photograph by the author.)

CAMP BENNING MARKER. This granite slab, presented by the Columbus Chamber of Commerce, was dedicated July 4, 1947, near the intersection of Macon Road and Dixon Drive, Columbus, in the presence of civilian and military leaders. Due to the widening of Macon Road, it was moved to the median of the intersection of Mimosa Street, and South Dixon Drive, on part of the original Camp Benning site. (Courtesy of the National Infantry Museum.)

Two

BEFORE THE ARMY

EMMAUS BAPTIST CHURCH. The United States Army's search for a permanent location for Camp Benning led to land nine miles south of Columbus. Condemnation proceedings on the land began in early 1919. Besides small farmsteads, the 97,000 acres eventually acquired in the first acquisition included schools, cemeteries, general stores, grist mills, and churches, such as this one, on Buena Vista Road. This *c.* 1890 view shows the assembled congregation. (Author's collection.)

SNELLINGS FAMILY ON PORCH. The family of Robert R. and Lenorah Johnson Snellings (couple on far right) is shown gathered for a family wedding on the back porch of the Johnson-Snellings home on Buena Vista Road on September 17, 1893. Little did they know that the tranquility of their rural community would be dramatically changed 25 years later by the arrival of the United States Army. (Original in the collection of the late Lillian S. Nicholson.)

SNELLINGS FAMILY GATHERING. Mrs. Lenorah Johnson Snellings (center, foreground) is shown with her family c. late 1920s. Her husband, a Civil War veteran, died in May 1918, and she was allowed a life estate on her farmstead, where she had been born in 1848. She died there, within the military reservation, in 1940. The author's mother, Louise Brooks, is to the right of Mrs. Snellings. (Original in the collection of the late Lillian S. Nicholson.)

FARMER'S HOUSE. This house is typical of the many small farmhouses on the land condemned by the U.S. government to create Fort Benning. Many land owners accepted the government's appraisals, took the money, and moved. The houses of those who awaited a U.S. District Court decision on the value were photographed, as was this one. (Courtesy of Dan Elliott, original in the National Archives and Records Administration, Southeast Region, Atlanta.)

MOTLEY FAMILY CEMETERY. The many small family and church cemeteries within the land acquired for Fort Benning are maintained by the military. This view is of the author's visit c. 1963 to the graves of his ancestors, Thomas Motley (1792–1861) and Lourina Barbee Motley (1790–1853), near Randall Creek, Muscogee County. Shown from left to right are an unidentified man, Joe Brooks, J. Mike Hostinsky, and Helen Russell Brooks. The Brookses were the author's grandparents. (Author's Collection.)

EELBECK MILL. The Eelbeck grist mill, shown in this 1940s postcard, was originally established by Henry J. Eelbeck. The mill pond was a favorite swimming spot for some. The mill was owned and operated by C.R. and Rosa King Mehaffey who sold the land to the government in 1920 and ran the mill until 1943. (Courtesy of John Mallory Land.)

MEHAFFEY FAMILY. This 1938 view shows C.R. and Rosa King Mehaffey and family in their home near the Eelbeck mill property. After the house and mill were sold to the government, they continued to live there until 1943. By then, with World War II well underway, the military had expanded Fort Benning in 1941 with more acreage in a second acquisition. (Courtesy of Lucile Mehaffey Rushin Hunter.)

CULPEPPER'S STORE. This *c.* 1941 interior view of the E.H. Culpepper General Store shows Mr. Pedrue Culpepper and his daughter-in-law, Mrs. Essie Sizemore Culpepper, holding her son, Ennon Jr. This store, located on Buena Vista Road, was acquired by the government in the second, or 1941, acquisition. (Original owned by Ennon H. Culpepper, Jr., courtesy of John Mallory Land.)

A SCHOOL. This school is associated with either Emmaus Baptist Church (see above) or Midway Methodist Church, both on Buena Vista Road, Muscogee County. In the early 20th century before the advent of modern consolidated schools, there were many such one-room school houses. These children and their teachers would have lived nearby. (Gift of the late Martha Ritch Magoni Foster.)

ARTHUR BUSSEY. The Bussey Plantation, the 1,750-acre dairy farm and second home of Arthur and Starlight Bussey of Columbus, was taken over in late 1918 for the location of the Main Post area of Camp Benning. Located in Chattahoochee County just across Upatoi Creek from Muscogee County, the Bussey Place included "Riverside," a house built in 1909. The nearest post office was Shack, Georgia. (Courtesy of Sally Bickerstaff Hatcher, granddaughter of the Busseys.)

BUSSEY REUNION AT RIVERSIDE. "Riverside," the Bussey's main house at their plantation, became the commanding general's residence. Many of the descendants of the Busseys, including the Bickerstaffs, Hatchers, and Woolfolks, are shown here on July 28, 2001, with Maj. Gen. and Mrs. John M. LeMoyne, the Infantry School Commandant and his wife, the residents of the house. The photograph was taken by Sgt. Samantha Torres for *The Bayonet*. (Courtesy of Sally Bickerstaff Hatcher, granddaughter of the Busseys.)

BUSSEY FAMILY REUNION
RIVERSIDE
JULY 28, 2001

Three

MAIN POST

1919–1920s

TENTS AS HOUSING. Camp Benning moved in June 1919 to the permanent encampment on Main Post. Officers and enlisted men were housed in tents erected on farmland as in this *c.* 1925 photo of tents near a silo said to be on the former W.C. Bradley property that adjoined Bussey's on the west. Many early officers' wives lived with them in tents. (Courtesy of the Georgia Division of Archives and History and the National Infantry Museum.)

MAIN POST, 1921. This January 1921 aerial view of the new encampment shows the tents as well as the wooden buildings that were quickly erected by the summer and fall of 1919. (Courtesy of the National Infantry Museum.)

MAIN POST, 1920. This aerial view appeared on one of the earliest postcards of Camp Benning, although no photographer or publisher is named. The railroad tracks are in the lower left with the main buildings and tents in the foreground and other buildings to the right. (Author's collection.)

WOODEN ENCAMPMENT. This photo takes a closer look, c. 1919, at the large number of two-story wooden buildings that were erected within the first six months of Camp Benning's move to the new Main Post location. The railroad tracks are in the lower portion of the photograph. (Published in *The Industrial Index, Fort Benning Number, October 30, 1940,* Author's collection.)

VISITING THE BOYS AT CAMP BENNING. This postcard and the one on the following page were both published by a national postcard publisher. It was mailed in September 1920 with a Columbus postmark. The series was issued as part of a United States Army set that showed similar buildings that represented Army bases in general. (Author's collection.)

HEADQUARTERS STAFF. Col. Henry E. Eames was the first commandant of the Infantry School at both the Macon Road site and the new location. This February 1920 photo shows him (far left) with Maj. Gen. Charles Farnsworth(center), the second commandant, and an unidentified officer in front of the Infantry School Headquarters building, shown in the postcard on the next page. (Courtesy of the National Infantry Museum.)

SKIRMISH LINE DRILL AT CAMP. This postcard, like the one on the preceding page, was published by the same national publisher for the Army and represents typical Army base wooden buildings and a typical drill. Although it was postmarked in November 1919 and mailed from Camp Benning, it is not certain that it represents an actual view of Camp Benning. The soldier who mailed the card commented "This is some warm climate." (Courtesy of Mike Helms.)

HEADQUARTERS, THE INFANTRY SCHOOL. This postcard shows the new headquarters of the Infantry School in 1919 at the new Main Post location. The building was used for classrooms and staff offices until it burned in September 1924. In 1925 the Infantry School activities were moved to the building shown below. This postcard was published by C.A. Stead of New Orleans. (Author's collection.)

HEADQUARTERS, THE INFANTRY SCHOOL. This building was originally a creamery on the Bussey Plantation dairy farm and today is Building 5 on Vibbert Avenue, just behind "Riverside," the Commandant's Quarters. This building was refurbished in 1925 and was used as the Infantry School Headquarters until the new headquarters building opened in 1935. It has been expanded and is now (as Winship Hall) used by the office of the Staff Judge Advocate. (Author's collection.)

OFFICERS' QUARTERS. This is a 1925 view of one of the many buildings built for officers' residences in the initial buildup *c.* 1919 to the 1920s. (Courtesy of the Georgia Division of Archives and History and the National Infantry Museum.)

First Lieutenant
JEFFERSON DENMAN BOX
U. S. M. A., 1920
Vernon, Alabama
"Jeff"   "Alonzo"   "Colonel"

U. S. M. A., 1918–1920.

S-s-s-snake. That fully describes this black-haired, heart-breaking "Son of Alabama." He claims that he is indifferent, and maybe so, but few are the nights that "Jeff" pulls in before the new day starts. Where does he go? you ask. Well, it is no particular one. He plays them all with the determination to reach his objective, which has been excelled in the past only by such men as Grant, Lee and "Baron" Duffner.

To put "Jeff" in a nutshell, we have him not with the motto, "Wine, women and song," but "No work, some women, and more sleep."

LT. JEFF BOX. Camp Benning brought many men to the Columbus area who remained in the community. Jeff Box, shown here in his 1920–1921 entry in *The Doughboy*, the Infantry School yearbook, was one of the earliest to do so. After his military service, he returned to Columbus and remained there until his death in 1979. Box Road which led to his home is named for him. (From *The Doughboy*, 1920–1921, Author's collection.)

THE INFIRMARY. This is a view of the early medical facility on post before the permanent station hospital opened in 1925. The sign on the post reads "Hospital, No Thoroughfare." Note several patients on the right. For more serious illnesses, soldiers were taken to the Columbus City Hospital. (Courtesy of the National Infantry Museum.)

EARLY AVIATORS. This *c.* 1921 photograph shows a bi-plane and the Air Service officers who arrived at Camp Benning in May 1920. (From *The Doughboy*, 1920–1921, Author's collection.)

BIGLERVILLE, OFFICERS' OPEN MESS. This building was completed in 1921 as the Infantry School student officers' mess hall. It is now the oldest remaining major building built on post by the Army. Here George Patton received his brigadier general's star in 1940. Now it is Building 229, Crain Hall, the Officers' Spouses Club and is located on Ingersoll Avenue at Compton Street (Curt Teich postcard, Author's collection.)

Enlisted Men's Service Club, Columbus, Ga.—23

ENLISTED MEN'S SERVICE CLUB. Completed in 1920, this was one of the first two major permanent buildings built on post. Later, Doughboy Stadium and Gowdy Field were built on either side of it on Ingersoll Street. Another postcard had the caption: "This club is the center of enlisted men's activities after duty hours. Various types of entertainment are provided for them at the club, such as dances, plays, musical recordings, and concerts." It was demolished in the 1990s. (Author's collection.)

TROOPS BEING REVIEWED. These men stand in review in front of their tent quarters in this *c.* 1920s photograph. Their boots indicate they were part of a mounted unit, either artillery or cavalry. (Courtesy of the National Infantry Museum.)

GEN. JOHN J. PERSHING. General Pershing (1860–1948), hero of World War I, visited Camp Benning several times and is remembered for major local floods that coincided with his visits in 1919 and 1922. He participated in the groundbreakings for Doughboy Stadium and Gowdy Field. This photo, while he was Chief of Staff of the United States Army, was inscribed for the Infantry School and dated March 22, 1921. (From *The Doughboy*, 1920–1921, Author's collection.)

CEREMONY AT RIVERSIDE. Many of the early Infantry School graduation ceremonies and other events were held on the lawn of "Riverside," the former Bussey Plantation home, used after 1919 as the Commandant's Quarters. This oft-used photo has been identified as the Infantry School graduation ceremony of June 30, 1921. (Courtesy of the National Infantry Museum.)

FORMATION WITH BALLOON. This aerial view shows troops assembled on a parade ground, arranged to spell out the words "Infantry School, Camp Benning, GA. 1921." Note the balloon in the rear center; it was operated by the 32nd Balloon Company housed at what became Lawson Field. The photo was by Eastern News Photo Service of Washington, DC. (Courtesy of the Georgia Division of Archives and History and the National Infantry Museum.)

Four

MAIN POST

1930s

GREETINGS FROM FORT BENNING. Camp Benning was raised to the level of a fort on February 8, 1922. This c. 1942 postcard reflects many of the base's new activities, including the Parachute School, during World War II. (Author's collection.)

ENTRANCE GATES. The entrance gates to the main post have changed several times over the years. This postcard from a *c.* 1930s series displays them. After a second bridge was completed in May 1953, this entrance road became one-way and a second entrance road was added. (Courtesy of Mike Helms.)

NEW BRIDGE OVER UPATOI CREEK. This 1935 aerial view shows the new bridge near completion over Upatoi Creek, which separates Muscogee County in the lower foreground from Chattahoochee County and the main post buildings in the rear. Behind Outpost No. 1 the officers' quarters and the Cuartel Barracks can be seen. (United States Army photograph, Author's collection.)

OUTPOST NO. 1. The Provost Marshall's Outpost No. 1, the entrance guard station, was constructed in 1935—located just after one crossed Upatoi Creek on the new bridge into the Main Post area. The building was demolished in 1965. (From *A Camera Trip* [c. 1942], Author's collection.)

BETJEMAN BRIDGE. The new bridge over Upatoi Creek was named in February 1936 and dedicated in 1937 in honor of John A. Betjeman (1880–1924). He was sent to Washington in 1918 as the resident agent of the Columbus Chamber of Commerce to influence the Army to relocate the Infantry School of Arms to the Columbus area. A bronze plaque on the bridge light post honors him. (Courtesy of the National Infantry Museum.)

AERIAL VIEW OF MAIN POST. The Infantry School at the lower left and the Officers' Club behind it with the axis of Wold Street leading west past Gowdy Field toward the Cuartel Barracks are shown in this 1950s aerial view. (United States Army photograph from *The Industrial Index, Fort Benning Number, December 5, 1951*, Author's collection.)

INFANTRY SCHOOL, OFFICERS' CLUB, AND POST CHAPEL. This 1935 aerial view real-photo postcard, mailed in 1937, shows the juxtaposition of three of the most well-known buildings on post. Doughboy Stadium can be seen just behind the chapel. This view looks northwest. (Author's collection.)

FOLLOW ME INSIGNIA. This emblem has long been the Coat of Arms of the Infantry School. In 1921, Capt. Elbridge Colby wrote that the shield represents foot soldiers of old and is in infantry blue. The "argent" bayonet symbolizes "the battle won" and that the infantry would lead in battle. Thus, "If the bayonet could speak, what could it say but 'Follow Me.'" Since the Infantry School leads the infantry it says to the entire Army: "Follow Me." (Author's collection.)

THE INFANTRY SCHOOL. The Infantry School Building, completed in 1935, is shown c. 1950. It was designed by the prestigious New York firm of McKim, Mead, and White. In 1935 the mission of the school was stated to be "designed to impart to officers of the United States infantry the latest principles and tactics used in the art of modern warfare and the course of instruction has been arranged to that end." (Author's collection.)

THE INFANTRY SCHOOL, CLOSE UP. This is a view of the front of the Academic Building under construction on July 3, 1935. Courses of instruction at the school c. 1935 included lectures and demonstrations on how to handle troops and practical work by the student officers to put the theoretical in place by commanding demonstration troops in the field. (United States Army photograph, Author's collection.)

THE INFANTRY SCHOOL. This rear photograph of the Infantry School Building (Building 35) shows the Calculator monument. Infantry School functions were moved to the new Infantry School Building (Building 4) when it opened in 1964. In 1984, this building became headquarters for the United States Army's School of the Americas, later renamed the Western Hemisphere Institute for Security Cooperation. In 1994, this building was renamed Ridgway Hall in honor of Gen. Matthew B. Ridgway. (Author's collection.)

CALCULATOR MONUMENT. Calculator was a dog that endeared himself to the men stationed at Fort Benning. At his death in 1923 he was greatly mourned. The men took up a collection and had this monument erected in 1930 in front of the old Officers' Club. It was moved to the Infantry School rear entrance in 1935 and in 1984 was moved to the grounds of the National Infantry Museum. The inscription reads: "CALCULATOR /BORN ?/DIED AUG. 29, 1923/ HE MADE BETTER DOGS OF US ALL." (Author's collection.)

37

OLD AND NEW BARRACKS. This 1927 view shows three types of enlisted housing. In the foreground are the wooden barracks built *c.* 1919–1920, to the left the Cuartel Barracks that would eventually replace these buildings are under construction, and in the far distance is a vast sea of tents being used for housing. (Courtesy of the National Infantry Museum.)

CUARTEL BARRACKS. The Cuartel Barracks are one of the most impressive structures at Fort Benning. They consist of three sets of semi-circular buildings built from 1925 to 1939. The first portion, at far right, was for the 29th Infantry, the demonstration regiment, and the 1935 portion, at left here, was for the 24th Infantry, the African American regiment. This 1937 photograph shows the middle portion in the center of this photo. (Author's collection.)

Barracks on the Main Po[st]

RETREAT PARADE AT THE CUARTEL BARRACKS. This is a retreat parade on June 6, 1941, on the parade ground within one of the Cuartel Barracks. "Cuartel" is a Spanish word for barracks. (From *The Camera Trip* [c. 1942], Author's collection.)

TENTS INSIDE THE CUARTEL BARRACKS. Due to a shortage of housing as World War II approached, tents were used on the Cuartel Barracks parade ground, seen here in 1941. (Courtesy of the National Infantry Museum.)

AERIAL VIEW, 1941. This aerial view and the image on the following page are part of a 41-inch long panoramic view of the base taken in 1941 by Vernon Oliver. For many years, Vernon and his father, Christian Oliver, who was born in Iceland, worked as civilian photographers at various military bases. While living in Columbus they photographed graduating classes from the various training units from 1941 to 1943 using a circuit camera. In these photographs one sees,

on the left, the easternmost Cuartel Barracks unit with a large section of tents in the right foreground used as living quarters during the overflow of troops during the buildup before World War II. In the photo at right, one can see the Main Post Chapel and the Main Post Theater in the distance. (Courtesy of Christal Oliver Speer.)

LAWSON FIELD, EARLY HANGARS. These hangars, shown in a May 1935 aerial photograph, were built *c.* 1920 as an observation balloon post for the 32nd Balloon Company and were where the first airplanes landed. Note the Flight C Tents to the left of the hangars and the biplanes on the field. These hangars at Lawson Field were upgraded many times. (United States Army photograph, Author's collection.)

LAWSON FIELD, 1935 HANGARS. This May 1935 aerial view shows the newly completed hangars just south of the ones pictured above. They are still in use at Lawson Field, which was named in 1931 for Capt. Walter R. Lawson, a World War I veteran killed in an airplane crash in 1923. (United States Army photograph, Author's collection.)

Five

TRAINING

INFANTRY SCHOOL GREETINGS. This *c.* 1940s postcard showcased various landmarks of Fort Benning as well as the most famous training units, the Infantry School and the Parachute School. (Curt Teich postcard, Author's collection.)

The U. S. Infantryman of Today--at Fort Benning

INFANTRYMAN, 1940. This infantryman is wearing the uniform still being used in 1940 with the 1917 A-1 helmet with chin strap and the M-1 rifle. The man was a member of the 29th Infantry Regiment. The helmet and other aspects of the uniform changed just after the United States entered World War II a little over a year later. (From *The Industrial Index, Fort Benning Number, October 30, 1940,* Author's collection.)

INFANTRYMEN ON REVIEW. This *c.* 1940 photograph of soldiers on review also displays the uniform and helmets used between the World Wars. (From *Fort Benning, Georgia* [*c.*1944], Author's collection.)

MILITARY REVIEW. Brig. Gen. Asa Singleton, Infantry School commandant, on horseback, second from left, reviews tanks and airplanes at Gordon Field most likely as part of his retirement ceremony in August 1940. Singleton, born in Taylor County, Georgia, in 1876, served earlier as colonel of the 29th Infantry Regiment. He died in 1943. (Courtesy of the Georgia Division of Archives and History and the National Infantry Museum.)

MILITARY REVIEW. For this 1941 event former commandant Brig. Gen. (Ret.) Asa Singleton returns in civilian clothes to review the troops in formation at the Infantry School Building. (Courtesy of the National Infantry Museum.)

THE INFANTRY BOARD 1940-41

FRONT ROW L TO R— LT. COL. S. T. WILLIAMS; LT. COL. H. M. MELASKY; LT. COL. R. O. BALDWIN; COL. S. H. MACGREGOR, (ORD.); BRIG. GEN. OMAR BRADLEY; BRIG. GEN. C. H. HODGES, COMMANDANT, T.I.S. AND PRESIDENT, T. I. B.; COL. C. W. THOMAS, JR., ASST. COMDT. T.I.S.; LT. COL. T. F. TAYLOR, DIRECTOR; LT. COL. T. A. PEDLEY, JR.; LT. COL. G. O. MORROW; MAJ. P. E. GALLAGHER.

REAR ROW L TO R.— 1ST LT. O. J. ALLEN; CAPT. W. C. RUTHERFORD; CAPT. J. W. HAMMOND; MAJ. E. A. CHAZAL; MAJ. K. MAERTENS; MAJ. H. G. SYDENHAM; MAJ. W. S. TRIPLETT; CAPT. I. R. CLARK; 1ST LT. R. E. SMITH.

ABSENT — LT. COL. R. MARSH, (ORD. DEPT.); LT. COL. J. L. READY.

THE INFANTRY BOARD. The Infantry Board, established at Fort Benning from 1919 until 1991, tested new products and set standards for the infantry. This 1940–1941 view of the Infantry School includes, front row, fifth from left, Brig. Gen. Omar Bradley, soon to be Infantry School commandant, and, sixth from left, Brig. Gen. Courtney H. Hodges, outgoing commandant. A historical marker at Building 76, on Anderson Street, marks the board's last headquarters. (Courtesy of the National Infantry Museum.)

CIVILIAN STAFF. In November 1942 these ladies were each a secretary to one of the generals: (from left to right) Mrs. Emma Price (Brig. Gen. George H. Weems, assistant commandant of the Infantry School); Mrs. Sue Irvin Woodall, (Brig. Gen. George Howell, of the Parachute School); and Mrs. Nelle Freeman (confidential secretary to the post commanding general, Brig. Gen. Walter S. Fulton, in whose office they are posing). Note the general's one star flag. (United States Army photograph, courtesy of Ms. Susan Woodall-Stuckey.)

YOU ARE IN THE ARMY NOW. In 1941, these young men standing near the Cuartel Barracks raise their right hands to be sworn into the United States Army. (Courtesy of the National Infantry Museum.)

BLACKS ENLISTING. In this 1940s photograph a group of African Americans are joining the Army at the country's largest "colored reception center." The white and black troops were separated in the Army until well after it was integrated in 1948. At Fort Benning this meant separate barracks, other housing, and even separate motion picture theaters. (From *The Camera Trip* [c.1942], Author's collection.)

MARCHING THROUGH THE TENTS. These African-American soldiers are marching down the company street past a row of tents at the "colored reception center" where they lived due to the lack of housing. Note the Cuartel Barracks in the rear. Troops of the all-black 24th Infantry, stationed at Benning since the 1920s, were housed in the portion of the Cuartel completed in 1935. (Courtesy of the National Infantry Museum.)

Basketball team of G. Co. 24ht Inf.
August 10,1928

BASKETBALL TEAM. This was the basketball team of G Company, 24th Infantry, photographed on August 10, 1928. L. Albert Scipio identifies them in his book *The 24th Infantry at Fort Benning* (1986) as, left to right, H. Williams (?), unidentified, ? Richell, ? Powell, L. Tillis, ? Trammell, S. Williams, and ? DeCuir. (Courtesy of the National Infantry Museum.)

SOLDIERS POSE. These African-American soldiers pose for the camera in the 1940s at either the Sand Hill or Harmony Church cantonment areas. (Courtesy of the National Infantry Museum.)

THE SALUTE. In 1947, a unit of African-American soldiers of the 1st Battalion, 25th Infantry Regiment, received the colors. (Courtesy of the National Infantry Museum.)

OBSTACLE COURSE. These men train by running through an obstacle course, *c.* 1942. (From *The Camera Trip* [*c.*1942], Author's collection.)

OBSTACLE COURSE. Another view of the obstacle course shows these men, with rifles, having to cross a man-made pond as part of training, *c.* 1942. The caption reads: "The obstacle course helps toughen up our new Army." (From *The Camera Trip* [*c.* 1942], Author's collection.)

FIELD KITCHEN. Food is served to the men in the field while training. (From *The Camera Trip* [*c.* 1942], Author's collection.)

AT THE MOVIES. These men are assembled to watch a "recreational film." (Courtesy of the National Infantry Museum.)

LEAVING THE SCHOOL. These officers leave the Infantry School after a training session. (From *The Camera Trip* [c.1942], Author's collection.)

OUTDOOR CLASSROOM. These Officer Candidate School (O.C.S.) candidates are at an outdoor classroom. (From *The Camera Trip* [c. 1942], Author's collection.)

GRADUATION. This unidentified officer has just graduated and is having his rank pinned on him by presumably his mother on the left and his wife on the right. This scene has certainly been repeated thousands of times over the years at Fort Benning. (Courtesy of the National Infantry Museum.)

ROTC. College Reserve Officer Training Corps (ROTC) cadets have been coming to Fort Benning since 1927. This 1962 yearbook cover highlights some of the colleges who sent students during that summer. (Author's collection.)

MILITARY REVIEW. This *c.* 1940 review is taking place on the parade grounds inside the Cuartel Barracks. (Courtesy of the National Infantry Museum.)

MILITARY REVIEW. An overview of the type of military reviews held outside the east entrance sally port of the Cuartel Barracks at Stillwell Field is shown in this picture. This is a full-scale event with the general in attendance; note the one-star flag in right foreground. (Courtesy of the National Infantry Museum.)

MARCH IN REVIEW. These soldiers are marching in a 1939 review on the parade grounds inside the Cuartel Barracks. (Courtesy of the National Infantry Museum.)

A FORMATION. This 1940 formation is also on the parade grounds within the Cuartel Barracks. (Courtesy of the National Infantry Museum.)

55

TANK CLASS—1939-40

Top Row. Left to Right:
LT. CHING YANG LIU. LT. LANDRUM. LT. SNYDER. LT. KELLY. LT. HAWES. LT. RICHARDSON. LT. COX. LT. ISHAM. LT. SKELLS.

Second Row. Left to Right:
LT. WRIGHT. LT. CUMMINGS. LT. GLASS. LT. BREARLEY. LT. THROCKMORTON. LT. ANDRAE. LT. FULLER. LT. BLANCHARD. LT. SCOVILLE. LT. BAILEY. LT. AKERS. LT. TALBOT. LT. COCHRAN.

Bottom Row. Left to Right:
LT. BUSE (USMC). LT. HERRICK. LT. MARNANE. CAPT. FADNESS. CAPT. CRUISE. MAJ. BRAGG. LT. COL. HARRISON. MAJ. BURACKER. CAPT. HAMMACK. CAPT. COOK (USMC). CAPT. GRIFFITH. CAPT. ALDERMAN.

Note: CAPT. PEPLOE not present when picture was taken.

TANK CLASS, 1939–1940. Officers of various ranks, including some foreign officers and some marines, pose in front of a tank outside the Cuartel Barracks in 1940. The Tank School transferred to Fort Benning in 1932. (Courtesy of the National Infantry Museum.)

TANKS READY FOR ACTION. This United States Army Signal Corps 1943 postcard shows the more modern tank used in World War II. (Curt Teich postcard, Author's collection.)

SECOND ARMORED DIVISION REVIEW, 1941. On February 14, 1941, the large Second Armored Division Review was held; 2,000 motor vehicles and 10,000 men participated. (Courtesy of the National Infantry Museum.)

ARMORED DIVISION IN REVIEW, FORT BENNING, GEORGIA—38

2ND ARMORED DIVISION REVIEW. This is a postcard of the 1941 mass review showing trucks pulling artillery. (Author's collection.)

ARMORED DIVISION OFFICERS. Taken in the Sand Hill area, this January 1943 photograph is of the headquarters staff of the Tenth Armored Division, known as "the Tigers." In this central portion of a 36-inch photo taken by photographer Christian Oliver, Maj. Gen. Paul J. Newgarden, commander, is shown right center. He was killed in a plane crash in 1944. (Courtesy of Christal Oliver Speer.)

SAND HILL AREA. This August 1941 aerial view of the Sand Hill area shows the large number of barracks and other buildings of the cantonment built for the Second Armored Division that arrived at Fort Benning in 1940. (Courtesy of the National Infantry Museum.)

A Sergeant on his Armored Vehicle.
Technical Sgt. Albert J. Komantoskas of
Forest City, Pennsylvania, is shown atop an
armored half/track vehicle. Komantoskas was a
member of the Second Armored Division and
trained at Fort Benning from March 1941 until
July 1942 before going to North Africa. He
now lives in Atlanta, Georgia. (Courtesy of
Alan J. Koman.)

Patton Addresses the Troops. George S.
Patton came to Fort Benning as a colonel
in July 1940. In October 1941, Patton, by
then a major general, addressed this large
assembly of men of the Second Armored
Division, which he commanded, at the
amphitheater at Sand Hill. (Courtesy of the
National Infantry Museum.)

FIELD ARTILLERY. This 1939 postcard shows men using the weapons of the 83rd Field Artillery. (Curt Teich postcard, Author's collection.)

BIVOUAC IN THE WOODS. The soldiers pictured are setting up for an overnight camp exercise on the Fort Benning reservation, *c.* 1939. There are tents, wagons, and horses. (Courtesy of the Georgia Division of Archives and History and the National Infantry Museum.)

Trucks Cross the Pontoon Bridge. This *c.* 1941 postcard shows Army trucks of the 20th Engineers crossing the pontoon bridge on the Chattahoochee River. The caption indicates they are from the Corps of Engineers and are constructing the bridge. (Author's collection.)

Pontoon Bridge. This *c.* 1926 photograph shows a pontoon bridge built across the Chattahoochee River. (Courtesy of the Georgia Division of Archives and History and the National Infantry Museum.)

WACS. Members of the Women's Army Corps are assembled in front of their barracks to receive an "Award of Merit" unit citation in 1946. Women soldiers first arrived at Fort Benning in 1943. (Courtesy of the National Infantry Museum.)

WOMEN AT WORK. These four members of the WACS are shown in an office in 1944. They are identified, from left to right, as Maj. Emily C. Davis, Maj. Margaret Craighill, PFC Verda Kragh, and Capt. Jean Melin. (Courtesy of the National Infantry Museum.)

WEST POINT CADETS. These West Point cadets (class of 1942) are shown in 1941 at Fort Benning. From left to right, kneeling, are Lawrence A. Adams, ? Hill, A.E. Frawley, and an unidentified sergeant. Standing at right are Charlie George and Edgar B. Colladay. Standing at rear with binoculars is Don Simon. (Identification by Col. [Ret.] James Hayes, United States Military Academy Class of 1942, Courtesy of the National Infantry Museum.)

CADETS WITH DATES. This summer 1946 photo shows two West Point cadets in uniform with a civilian and their three dates at "Riverside," the Commandant's Quarters. This scene was repeated frequently as cadets had been coming to Fort Benning for decades before and since, and some married local Columbus women. (Courtesy of the National Infantry Museum.)

O.C.S Candidate Reports In. This c.1941 photo shows a sergeant reporting for Officer Candidate School (O.C.S.). (From *Fort Benning, Georgia [c. 1944]*, Author's collection.)

O.C.S. Insignia. The O.C.S. insignia was an intertwined C and S within the letter O in olive drab on a dark blue background. Fort Benning began its first O.C.S. class in July 1941. Since 1973 it has been the United States Army's only O.C.S. training center. The O.C.S. Hall of Fame was established in 1958 and is located in Wigle Hall on Riordon Street. (Courtesy of Mary Lewis Pierson.)

O.C.S. BARRACKS. The O.C.S. barracks in the Harmony Church area are shown *c.* 1942. in a photograph by Christian Oliver. (Courtesy of Christal Oliver Speer.)

O.C.S. GROUP PICTURE. This O.C.S. graduating class is the central portion of a 36-inch photo taken by Christian Oliver between 1941 and 1943. Oliver and his son, Vernon, photographed the graduating troops using a circuit camera with a wide-angle lens. The World War II O.C.S. program is the subject of *The Ninety-Day Wonders* (2001) by Milton M. McPherson; the author used the program's nickname as the book's title. (Courtesy of Christal Oliver Speer.)

RANGERS IN ACTION. This *c.* 1965 postcard shows Army Rangers training with an 81 mm mortar. The Rangers first came to Fort Benning in 1950. There is a Ranger Hall of Fame and Museum on post. (Author's collection.)

RANGERS CLIMBING. These Rangers wearing black berets train by climbing the cargo net at the O.C.S. obstacle course. (Columbus Photo Service postcard, Author's collection.)

RANGERS IN THE PIT. This *c.* 1960 view shows Rangers practicing around and in a pit. (Courtesy of the National Infantry Museum.)

RANGERS IN THE SWAMP. Rangers practice with weapons in a swamp. The caption on this postcard reads: "Ranger School, Patrolling Techniques. 'Ranger training is probably the best leadership training in the United States Army' Brig. General Robert Timothy." (Columbus Photo Service postcard, Author's collection.)

DOUGHBOY STATUE. The Doughboy Statue was placed in front of the Infantry School and dedicated in 1958. The nine foot bronze depicts a World War II Infantryman in full combat dress. The model was Staff Sgt. Thomas E. Love. Later it was moved to the west side of the new Infantry School Building (Building 4). The photograph was taken by George Ovitt. (Columbus Photo Service postcard, Author's collection, gift of Paula Harris.)

DOUGHBOY STATUE. The Doughboy Statue is shown here when it was in front of the old Infantry School (Building 35). The statue, a 1958 replica of the American Doughboy Statue in Berlin, was reproduced with contributions from Infantrymen worldwide. The plaque calls it "The American Infantryman" and indicates the six stones at the base are from the Bridge at Remagen, Germany, over the Rhine River, captured on March 7, 1945. (Courtesy of the Georgia Division of Archives and History and the National Infantry Museum.)

NEW INFANTRY SCHOOL. The new Infantry School center and headquarters building, now Building 4, was dedicated on June 5, 1964. The building covers 12 acres and is 6 stories high. The Infantryman/Follow Me statue is shown in front. (Columbus Photo Service postcard, courtesy of Mike Helms.)

NEW INFANTRY SCHOOL. The new 1964 building was built facing York Field, named for Sgt. Alvin York, World War I Medal of Honor winner. The Jump Towers can be seen behind the building. Known as Infantry Hall, it houses administrative offices, classrooms, and the Donovan Library. (Columbus Photo Service postcard, Author's collection.)

INFANTRYMAN STATUE. This statue was originally unveiled on May 3, 1960 at Eubanks Field before the new Infantry School headquarters was built. Eugene J. Wyles, then in O.C.S., modeled for the statue in 1959. It was originally known as the Infantryman Statue, as the caption reads on this card. It became known as the Follow Me statue, as it is on later postcards, after it was moved. The photograph was taken by George Ovitt. (Columbus Photo Service postcard, Author's collection.)

FOLLOW ME STATUE. On June 14, 1976, the 201st birthday of the United States Army, Infantry School commandant Maj. Gen. Willard Latham addressed the crowd at the annual ceremony. Standing beside him is James W. Woodruff Jr., of Columbus, who spearheaded the expansion of the National Infantry Museum. Woodruff died only a few months after this ceremony due to a car wreck. (Courtesy of the National Infantry Museum.)

Six

THE PARACHUTE
SCHOOL

THE JUMP TOWERS. This is a rare photo showing the four parachute jump towers at Eubanks Field. The first two—one captive, one free—were completed in May 1941, the third in November 1942, and the fourth in December 1942. Today only three survive, as the November 1942 one (in the center here) was destroyed by a tornado on March 13, 1954. This photo was taken by Jack Lieberman in 1944. (Courtesy of the Georgia Division of Archives and History and the National Infantry Museum.)

THE MOCK TOWER. Training begins in the 1960s as students perform a mass exit from the 34-foot Mock Tower. This procedure allowed the student to glide down a 200-foot cable after jumping and prepared the student for the shock of a jump. (Columbus Photo Service postcard, Author's collection.)

PREPARING FOR A JUMP. In 1942, Second Lt. Carl L. Patrick, a member of the Parachute School, prepares for a practice jump from one of the Mock Up Towers at Lawson Field. Patrick, who married Frances Wynn, a local woman, in 1943, returned to Columbus after overseas duty and was later president of Martin Theaters, and Carmike Cinemas. (Courtesy of Carl L. Patrick Sr. and Lewis P. Fern.)

PACKING THE PARACHUTES. One vital aspect of parachute training was learning to properly fold and pack your parachute and then using it in a jump. In this 1940s photo, students are in the packing shed learning the routine. (Courtesy of Carl L. Patrick Sr. and Lewis P. Fern.)

PRACTICING. In this 1941 photo, West Point cadet Jere W. Maupin, center, class of 1942, is in the T-5 parachute harness preparing for a practice jump below the controlled descent jump tower. He will land on a mattress to cushion his impact. On the far left is John A. Ely, and on the right, Carl W. Stapleton, both class of 1942. West Point cadets came to Fort Benning during the summer. (Courtesy of the Georgia Division of Archives and History and the National Infantry Museum.)

AT THE JUMP TOWER, GOING UP. Students and their parachutes were pulled up the 250-foot Jump Towers for a practice jump, as seen in this 1964 photograph by George Ovitt. (Columbus Photo Service postcard, Author's collection.)

MAKING A JUMP. This 1960s photograph shows students being dropped from the tower for a free-fall jump. This was a preliminary step in training before one actually jumped from an airplane. The building underneath the jump tower housed four elevator motors which raised the jumpers through cables and holes in the roof. The "Buttons Sergeant" sat in the cupola and operated the buttons which raised the jumpers. The photograph was taken by Jack Taylor. (Columbus Photo Service postcard, Author's collection.)

THE WIND MACHINE. A student is learning how to react to the pull of the parachute once he hits the ground in this 1943 photograph. The wind machine, made by the Wincharger Company of Sioux City, Iowa, housed a large fan. (Courtesy of the National Infantry Museum.)

PARACHUTE SCHOOL STAFF, 1942. Pictured from left to right are (front row) Capt. Richard Seitz; Capt. Morris Anderson, intelligence officer; Maj. Ward Ryan; Brig. Gen. George Howell, commanding general; Maj. John Nilan, supply officer (later a judge in Columbus); and Capt. Arthur Raber, adjutant; (back row) Lt. Walter Woirolt; Capt. Benj. Houston, area operation officer; Second Lt. Clarence West, assistant supply officer; Second Lt. Benj. McLean, range officer; First Lt. John Leary, custodial officer; and Capt. Benjamin Vandervoot, acting operation and training officer. (United States Signal Corps photo, courtesy of Ms. Susan Woodall-Stuckey.)

FINAL BRIEFING. In this 1970s photograph at McCarthy Hall, located at Lawson Field, students get a final mass briefing before heading out on the tarmac to board for a live jump. Built *c.* 1941, the hall was demolished in 1998. (Courtesy of the Columbus State University Archives.)

LINING UP TO BOARD. Students sit on the tarmac at Lawson Field waiting to board C-47 aircraft for a jump in this *c.* 1943 postcard, made from a United States Signal Corps photo. (Author's collection.)

WAITING TO BOARD. Parachute School students of the 501st Battalion line up to board the plane for a jump with their parachutes on their backs in this early 1941 photo,. They are wearing the A-2 cloth helmets that were replaced later in 1941 with the Riddell plastic helmet, which resembled a football helmet. (Courtesy of the Georgia Division of Archives and History and the National Infantry Museum.)

BOARDING FOR THE FIRST LIVE JUMP. This *c.* 1960s postcard shows students boarding a C-119 United States Air Force plane for what the caption says is their first live jump, one of five qualifying jumps. (Columbus Photo Service postcard, Author's collection.)

PARACHUTE TROOPS LEAVING THE PLANE. As others line up in the doorway to follow, a single trainee jumps out of a C-39 airplane at 750 feet above the earth. The sender of this April 1942 postcard said he had seen 13 jump out at once. (Author's collection.)

A MASS JUMP. The final mass test jump of the Parachute Test Platoon on August 29, 1940, was attended by Gen. George C. Marshall, United States Army Chief of Staff, Secretary of War, Henry Stimson, and other VIPs. The test platoon (July to September 1940) was followed by the Parachute School from May 1942 until December 1945 during which the mass jump was an often seen sight. Mass jumps are still seen today at Fort Benning. (Author's collection.)

79

LANDING. "Paratrooper collapsing his parachute after a jump on Fryar Drop Zone." This 1960s photograph shows a landing at Fryar Field, a part of Fort Benning located across the Chattahoochee River in Russell County, Alabama, on land purchased in 1941 as part of the second acquisition. The Airborne Walk was dedicated in 1986 at Eubanks Field. (Columbus Photo Service postcard, Author's collection.)

PARACHUTIST BADGE. The basic parachutist badge was designed by Capt. (later Lt. Gen.) William P. Yarborough, a company commander in the 501st, and cast in silver by Bailey, Banks & Biddle Company of Philadelphia. The 501st Parachute Battalion ordered the first batch in March 1941. The insignia was published in *Life*, June 9, 1941, following a May 12 article that stressed the all-volunteer nature of the United States parachute training program. (Courtesy of the National Infantry Museum.)

Seven

POST HOUSING

CUARTEL BARRACKS ENTRANCE. This impressive east entry sally port leads to the oldest one of the Cuartel Barracks, begun in 1925 for the enlisted men of the 29th Infantry Regiment, the demonstration unit. This entrance faces onto Gillespie Street and Stillwell Field. The photograph was taken by Jack Lieberman. (From *The Infantry School, Fort Benning, Georgia* [1944], Author's collection.)

CUARTEL BARRACKS. This postcard depicting the east side and oldest part of the Cuartel Barracks shows the massive nature of this three- and four-story building. (Curt Teich postcard, Author's collection.)

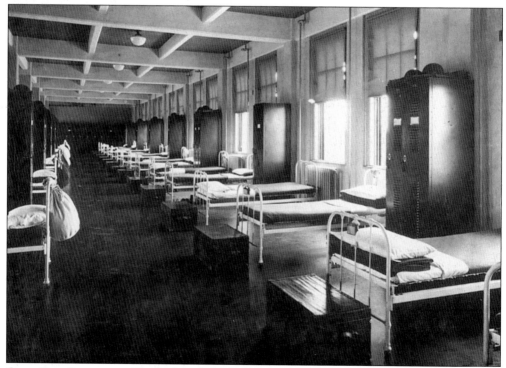

OPEN BAY BARRACKS. The beds and the lockers in the enlisted men's barracks are shown in this c.1928 photograph. (Courtesy of the Georgia Division of Archives and History and the National Infantry Museum.)

READY FOR INSPECTION. Here, an enlisted man's clothes and gear are laid out in full field display on his bunk in preparation for an inspection. (Courtesy of the National Infantry Museum.)

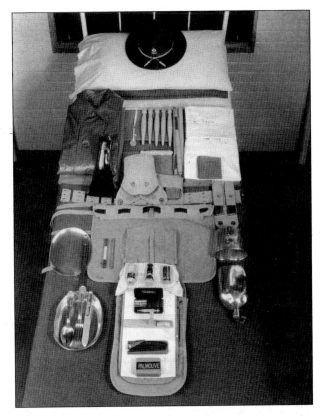

BARRACKS AT SAND HILL. During the buildup of troops at Fort Benning before and during World War II, the Sand Hill area became, in 1940, the home of the Second Armored Division. This view is typical of the many barracks that were built in that area. (From *The Industrial Index, Fort Benning Number, October 30, 1940*, Author's collection.)

INDIVIDUAL QUARTERS. These small officers' quarters were built due to the shortage of good base housing. Tents could be placed over similar ones, as shown below. (Author's collection.)

INDIVIDUAL QUARTERS. These small quarters, described above, are shown here covered with tents for privacy. (From *Fort Benning, Georgia* [c. 1944], Author's collection.)

1950s BARRACKS. This 1960s photograph shows the more modern enlisted men's barracks built in 1954 on Riordon Street next to the jump towers. (Courtesy of the Georgia Division of Archives and History and the National Infantry Museum.)

BOQs. These three buildings were built in 1934 as the Bachelor Officers Quarters, for single officers. Known from left to right as Lewis, Greene, and Collins Halls, they are on Richardson Circle and are shown here in a 1935 aerial view. Note the base hospital in the upper left and other base housing in the upper right. The field in front is now Honor Field and has the POW monument in the center. (United States Army photograph, Author's collection.)

OFFICERS QUARTERS. These Dutch Colonial style quarters, located today along Austin Loop and Eames Avenue, were built in 1923–1924 as the first permanent married officer housing for field officers. It was in a house of this style that Maj. Dwight D. Eisenhower and family lived in 1926–1927 while he was stationed at Fort Benning. A Historic Chattahoochee Commission historical marker on Vibbert Avenue commemorates their former unit at 206 Austin Loop. (From *The Industrial Index, Columbus Number, August 31, 1927*, Author's collection.)

OFFICERS QUARTERS. This *c.* 1935 photograph shows the type of housing originally built in 1935 for the student company grade officers, lieutenants, and captains. Each building has four apartments in it. They can be found today along First Division Road. (Courtesy of the Georgia Division of Archives and History and the National Infantry Museum.)

RAINBOW ROW. These Officers Quarters were built in 1932 on Rainbow Avenue near the base hospital (now the National Infantry Museum) and were painted alternating pastel colors. (Author's collection.)

OFFICERS QUARTERS. This 1935 photo shows a single-family dwelling for field grade officers, majors, lieutenant colonels, and colonels. These are still in use today and can be found at several locations, including Baltzell Avenue near the golf course. (Courtesy of the Georgia Division of Archives and History and the National Infantry Museum.)

OFFICERS QUARTERS. Shown here is a row of Officers Quarters, located along Lumpkin Road on the entrance/exit to the base across from "Riverside," Quarters One. Built in the early 1930s, they are still used today. (Curt Teich postcard, Author's collection.)

RIVERSIDE. This is the home of the commanding general of the Infantry School and is known as the Commandant's Quarters or Quarters One. The commandant and his family have resided here since the house was purchased along with the Bussey Plantation from Arthur Bussey in 1919 to form the core of the Main Post portion of Fort Benning. The house was built in 1909. (Author's collection.)

Eight

POST ACTIVITIES

MAIN POST CHAPEL. This chapel was completed in April 1935 for Catholic, Protestant, and Jewish worship. This Georgian Colonial Revival style building was designed by Columbus-native Philip Trammell Shutze for his firm, Hentz, Adler, and Shutze of Atlanta. The chapel, which seats 400, is still in use. (Author's collection.)

MAIN POST CHAPEL, REAR. This photo shows the rear of the Main Post Chapel. The design is similar to churches in Charleston, South Carolina. The main post chapel at Fort Bragg, North Carolina, is of the same design. A separate Catholic Chapel was built nearby in 1942 and recently burned. (Courtesy of the Georgia Division of Archives and History and the National Infantry Museum.)

MAIN POST CHAPEL, INTERIOR. The church's interior design reflects that of an 18th-century Episcopal church, such as one might find in Charleston, South Carolina. The minister would deliver the sermon from the pulpit at right. (Courtesy of the Georgia Division of Archives and History and the National Infantry Museum.)

MAIN POST CHAPEL SERVICE.
The congregation fills the
balconies during this church
service, *c.* 1940. The choir is in
the left foreground. (From *A
Camera Trip* [*c.* 1942], Author's
collection.)

A WEDDING. The Main Post
Chapel has been the scene for
many military weddings. In
this photo, Mary Frances Kelley
of Columbus has just wed
Maj. William F. Ahern of
Menominee, Michigan, and
they are proceeding through
the upraised sabers as they
leave the sanctuary on May 13,
1950. (Courtesy of Ms. Mary
Frances Ahern.)

HARMONY CHURCH CHAPEL. Built *c.* 1940 at the Harmony Church area of the base, this chapel is of the same design as numerous others built on U.S. military bases of that era. Others of this design were also built at Fort Benning. This chapel is the last surviving historic building in the Harmony Church area. (From *Fort Benning, Georgia* [*c.* 1944], Author's collection.)

IN CHURCH. The caption on this *c.* 1958 postcard reads: "Protestant Sunday Morning Worship, Harmony Church Chapel #1, 3D Infantry Division, Fort Benning, GA." The sender of the postcard stated that services were held on Sunday and Wednesday. (Author's collection.)

SIGHTSEEING ROAD CHAPEL. This more modern chapel was also called the First Infantry Brigade Chapel and was built c. 1956. It is located on Sightseeing Road at Way Street, next to the Audie Murphy Gym. (Columbus Photo Service postcard, Author's collection.)

SUNRISE SERVICES. The Horseshow Bowl, completed in 1930, is on the northwestern edge of Main Post near the Chattahoochee River. Originally built to show horses, it was later named for former commandant Maj. Gen. Campbell King. This 1930s view shows an Easter Sunrise Service held here for many years before World War II with as many as 10,000 attending, including many Columbus residents. The cross is made up of 1,200 soldiers. (Courtesy of the National Infantry Museum.)

A MILITARY FUNERAL. The funeral of Col. Frank Cole Baker, a surgeon, who was Hospital Commander when he died in his sleep on April 12, 1929, on post, is shown here. His casket, center, has just been escorted from the Catholic Chapel and is being placed on a caisson. Note the rider-less black horse and the assembled 29th Infantry troops. Colonel Baker was buried at Arlington National Cemetery. (Courtesy of the National Infantry Museum.)

MAIN POST CEMETERY. Begun in 1922, the cemetery is on the east side of Benning Boulevard before one crosses Upatoi Creek and enters the Main Post area. The tombstones are all the same size and style, without regard to rank or position. German and Italian POWs from World War II are also buried here. (Photograph by the author.)

DOUGHBOY MEMORIAL STADIUM. This football stadium was dedicated on October 17, 1925, followed by a game, Infantry vs. Oglethorpe University of Atlanta, before a crowd of 9,000. It was built from contributions raised by military units all over the world to honor the heroes of World War I. In 1924, Gen. John J. Pershing participated in the groundbreaking for the stadium. (From *The Industrial Index, Fort Benning Number, Dec. 5, 1951*, Author's collection.)

DOUGHBOY STADIUM. This postcard shows the ivy-covered stadium, hinting toward the "Ivy League," when it was the scene of football games played in the 1920s and 1930s between the Infantry team and regional colleges. The towers were added in 1929 and housed offices. The Post Exchange was also here for awhile. The stadium has been the scene of Easter Sunrise Services and of President Johnson's visit in 1967. (Curt Teich postcard, Author's collection.)

BASEBALL TEAM. The Infantry School's baseball team, shown here on April 12, 1927, played other military posts as well as college teams at Gowdy Field, below. (Courtesy of the National Infantry Museum.)

GOWDY FIELD. This baseball field was dedicated on March 31, 1925 and named for former Sgt. Hank Gowdy, a World War I veteran, who played that day for the New York Giants against the Washington Senators. Built from donations by servicemen, it is at the corner of Ingersoll Street and Wold Avenue. The Enlisted Man's Service Club (now demolished) was next to it. (Courtesy of the Georgia Division of Archives and History and the National Infantry Museum.)

SERVICE CLUBS. There were service clubs for enlisted men at several locations on post. This is an interior view of one in the Harmony Church area. The photograph was taken by Jack Lieberman. (From *The Infantry School, Fort Benning, Georgia* [1944], Author's collection.)

MAIN NCO SERVICE CLUB. This 1960s postcard shows the more recent Main Service Club built in 1964 for enlisted men. It is located on Sightseeing Road near Eckel Street. (Columbus Photo Service postcard, Author's collection.)

OFFICERS' CLUB. The main Officers' Club was completed in 1934 and is still in use today. It was built in the Spanish Mission Revival style, a style used in much of the officers' housing at Fort Benning. (Author's collection.)

OFFICERS' CLUB. This *c.* 1946 postcard of the Officers' Club shows the various additions made behind the building. The first swimming pool and a formal garden were added in 1937. The working drawings were prepared by Lorin D. Raines of Columbus. (Author's collection.)

OFFICERS' CLUB POOL. The swimming pool and pavilion at the Officers' Club are showcased in this photo. (Author's collection.)

OFFICERS' SUPPER CLUB. This *c.* 1960s postcard shows the new "ultra modern Supper Club, an addition to the Main Officer's Open Mess." It was built adjacent to the earlier club, seen at the left. This club was featured briefly in the movie *The Green Berets* filmed at Fort Benning in 1967. (Author's collection.)

POST EXCHANGE. This is a view of the main post exchange, *c.* 1940s. The architect was T. Firth Lockwood Jr., of Columbus. This photograph was taken by Christian Oliver. (Courtesy of Christal Oliver Speer.)

LIBRARIES. One of the many libraries located on post during World War II, the Second Armored Division library at Sand Hill is shown here in 1941. (Courtesy of the National Infantry Museum.)

GOLF HOUSE. This *c.* 1930 postcard by the Curt Teich Company shows the 1926 Golf House of the Officers' Club. Golf has been an integral part of Fort Benning since the earliest days. (Curt Teich postcard, Author's collection.)

BOY SCOUTS AND GIRL SCOUTS. This scout lodge photographed in 1944 was built in 1927 and was the center for Boy and Girl Scout activities. It has been demolished. The photo was taken by Jack Lieberman. (From *The Infantry School, Fort Benning, Georgia* [1944], Author's collection.)

THE CHILDREN'S SCHOOL. The Children's School was the first permanent school built on Main Post for white children. Built in 1931 on Baltzell Avenue, it was renamed the Patch School in 1959 for Capt. Alexander M. Patch III, United States Military Academy class of 1942, the son of Gen. Alexander "Sandy" Patch. Now Patch Hall, it is used as a childcare center. (Photograph by the author.)

FAITH SCHOOL. The original Don C. Faith Elementary School opened in 1952 and was located on the east side of Ingersoll Street. Now gone, the name has been transferred to the Don C. Faith Middle School on the west side of Ingersoll. The school was named for Medal of Honor winner Lt. Col. Don C. Faith. (Author's collection.)

THE HUNT CLUB. Members of the Fort Benning Hunt Club are on horseback, c. 1927. The hunt club continues to be a Fort Benning institution. (Courtesy of the Georgia Division of Archives and History and the National Infantry Museum.)

POLO PLAYERS. Polo was an integral part of Fort Benning for several decades. This c. 1947 photograph shows several players in action. The polo playing fields are along First Division Road and are named for two early polo players who died, French Field dedicated in 1926 for First Lt. Harry W. French and Blue Field dedicated in 1934 for Capt. John W. Blue. (Courtesy of the National Infantry Museum.)

MAIN THEATER. The Main Theater opened in February 1926 during the early base buildup of the 1920s. The first talking picture was shown here on January 5, 1930. It was superseded by the theater below. (Courtesy of the Georgia Division of Archives and History and the National Infantry Museum.)

MAIN THEATER. This is the Main Theater that was built in 1939. Located at the corner of Wold Avenue and Ingersoll Street, it was torn down in the 1990s. The theater built in 1933 for the black troops of the 24th Infantry is still standing as Building 72 at Wold Avenue and Anderson Street. (Author's collection.)

THE SWIMMING POOL. This 1920s postcard shows people gathered on the banks of the outdoor swimming pool or pond. Note the Red Cross lifesaving board at left and the diving tower on the right. (Author's collection.)

10—Russ Pool, the Infantry School, Ft. Benning, Ga.

RUSS POOL. Russ Pond, *c.* 1938, began in 1919 when a dam was built for a swimming hole. By 1926 there was a beach and concrete stands for 400 and by 1932 there was a bathhouse. This was a favorite spot for enlisted personnel and their Columbus visitors. Although the bathhouse is gone and the pool closed, the site remains a recreation spot. It is located on the north side of Main Post off Clark Road, near the Lumpkin Road entrance. (Curt Teich postcard, Author's collection.)

A. S. F. Regional Hospital—Fort Benning, Georgia

POST HOSPITAL. The original main post hospital, or station hospital, was finished in 1925 and used until 1958. In 1977 it became the National Infantry Museum. (Author's collection.)

POST HOSPITAL. This 1935 aerial view shows the hospital with the additional buildings built as its needs expanded. While the main building is a museum, the auxiliary buildings have other uses today. The land in front of the hospital, open again as in this view, is known as Sacrifice Field and contains monuments to various units. Note the golf course on the right, and Rainbow Row in the upper left. (United States Army photograph, Author's collection.)

MEDICAL CANTONMENT. Between the base buildup between 1940 and 1942, the area in front of the hospital was filled with temporary hospital buildings as shown in this 1941 aerial view. The hospital is shown in the upper right. These buildings were later torn down and most of the area is open ground again as in the previous picture. (Courtesy of the National Infantry Museum.)

MARTIN ARMY HOSPITAL. The caption on this 1960s postcard indicates that the hospital was built in 1958, had 500 beds, and cost $8 million. The nine-story building was named for Maj. Gen. Joseph I. Martin, Medical Corps, United States Army. It is still in use. The photograph was taken by George Ovitt. (Columbus Photo Service postcard, Author's collection.)

UNITED STATES ARMY INFANTRY MUSEUM. The United States Army Infantry Museum was opened on post in 1959 in a one-story building located on Ingersoll Street. After the museum, renamed the National Infantry Museum in 1975, was moved in 1977 to the old hospital, this building was reused for other purposes and was torn down in 1994. (Curt Teich postcard, Author's collection.)

NATIONAL INFANTRY MUSEUM DEDICATION. On July 1, 1977, the former hospital was dedicated as the National Infantry Museum. Gen. Omar N. Bradley was present and the building was named Bradley Hall in his honor. The building is still used as the museum. The grounds immediately in front of the museum contain monuments to various units, the Calculator monument, tanks, and the train. (Courtesy of the Georgia Division of Archives and History and the National Infantry Museum.)

THE TRAIN. This train was one of sixteen used from 1919 to 1946 to transport soldiers (as shown here) and construction materials around the post. It used a narrow gauge track. One nickname was the Chattahoochee Choo-Choo. The train was run by the Quartermaster Corps, hence the lettering on the engine. (Courtesy of the National Infantry Museum.)

THE LITTLE TRAIN. This 1960s postcard shows the remaining train engine and car that are now on the grounds of the National Infantry Museum, although this photo by George Ovitt shows the train on display at the intersection of Sigerfoos Road and Vibbert Avenue. (Columbus Photo Service postcard, Author's collection.)

2B-H560

THE U.S.O. CLUB. This building opened in May 1942, in downtown Columbus on the south side of Ninth Street, just across the street from the county courthouse. This postcard indicates that when it opened "It is one of the five largest of such clubs constructed in the United States." There were other clubs in Columbus, one especially for black servicemen and another run by the Masons. This building has been torn down. (Curt Teich postcard, Author's collection.)

U. S. O. CLUB
operated by
THE SALVATION ARMY

"The Writing Room"

SERVICEMEN AT A U.S.O. CLUB. Published by the Salvation Army's Atlanta headquarters, this card shows "The Writing Room" of a typical U.S.O. Club operated by the Salvation Army. Addressed to "Dear Sugar," the card was mailed "FREE" with a 1943 Fort Benning postmark. It is not certain if this is really a view of the U.S.O. Club in Columbus, or one used by the Salvation Army to represent any of their clubs. (Curt Teich postcard, Author's collection.)

Nine

VIPs

PRESIDENT HARDING. President Warren G. Harding came to Camp Benning on October 27, 1921, for a two-hour visit on a Southern tour that had included Birmingham and would go on to Atlanta. Pictured on the front row, from left to right, are Harding (with walking cane), Infantry School Commandant Maj. Gen. Walter H. Gordon, Secretary of War John W. Weeks, Secretary of the Interior Albert Fall, and Colonel Hanna. (Courtesy of the National Infantry Museum.)

MAJ. DWIGHT D. EISENHOWER. Eisenhower (in the A sweater) was stationed at Fort Benning briefly from 1926 to 1927, during which time he also coached a football team at Doughboy Stadium. The Eisenhowers lived at 206 Austin Loop, now marked with a historical marker from the Historic Chattahoochee Commission co-sponsored by the AUSA on Vibbert Avenue across from "Riverside." (Courtesy of the Georgia Division of Archives and History and the National Infantry Museum.)

EISENHOWER RETURNS. After leaving Fort Benning, Eisenhower advanced in his military career to become Supreme Allied Commander during World War II. In this April 7, 1947, photo he is touring the base as Chief of Staff of the United States Army. During his presidency, 1953 to 1961, he made four visits to Fort Benning, as his son was stationed there. His last visit as President was on May 3, 1960. (Courtesy of the National Infantry Museum.)

GEORGE S. PATTON. Patton arrived at Fort Benning in July 1940 as a colonel (shown here) and left in March 1942 as a major general. Although his tour of duty at the post was short, he left an indelible memory as commander of the Second Armored Division. He died due to an automobile accident in December 1945 in Germany just before he was to return to the states and was buried in Luxembourg. (Courtesy of the National Infantry Museum.)

PATTON HOME. General Patton and his wife Beatrice first lived on Main Post at 601 Baltzell Avenue, but built this house in 1941 in the Second Armored Division area at Sand Hill. After their departure in 1942, they gave it to the post and it became an Officers' Club. It burned on December 22, 1960. (Courtesy of the Georgia Division of Archives and History and the National Infantry Museum.)

OMAR N. BRADLEY IS SWORN IN. Omar Bradley is sworn in as a brigadier general by Lt. Col. Frank M. Smith, adjutant general of the Infantry School. Bradley, who had been at Fort Benning before as a student and later as an instructor, was commandant of the Infantry School from March 4, 1941, to February 10, 1942. He went on to command the United States forces for the D-Day Invasion in 1944 and became a 5-star General of the Army in 1950. (Courtesy of the National Infantry Museum.)

GENERAL BRADLEY RETURNS. General Bradley returned to Fort Benning for the dedication of the National Infantry Museum on July 1, 1977. He is shown on the steps of the old hospital which was renamed Bradley Hall in his honor. Left to right are Lt. Gen. Sam S. Walker, Mrs. Kitty Bradley, General Bradley, and Infantry School Commandant Maj. Gen. Willard Latham. General Bradley died in 1981. (Courtesy of the National Infantry Museum.)

GEN. GEORGE C. MARSHALL. George C. Marshall was assistant commandant of the Infantry School from 1927 to 1932 during which time he met his second wife, Katherine, at a dinner party in Columbus. Their house at 1st Division Road at Baltzell Avenue is marked with a historical sign. In this March 25, 1943 photo (from left to right) Sir Anthony Eden, British foreign secretary (in black coat), and Marshall, then Chief of Staff of the United States Army, tour the post. (Courtesy of the National Infantry Museum.)

RECEPTION FOR A VIP This photograph shows a typical military review and reception for an unidentified foreign VIP. (Courtesy of the National Infantry Museum.)

PRESIDENT ROOSEVELT IN 1938. Franklin D. Roosevelt visited Fort Benning as President in 1938 and 1943. On March 30, 1938, F.D.R. drove from Warm Springs to a large rally at the courthouse in Columbus, then to Fort Benning for a two-hour visit. He reviewed the troops at Gordon Field. From left to right are Lt. Col. L.P. Hunt, F.D.R, Georgia governor E.D. Rivers, and Mrs. Roosevelt. (From *The Industrial Index, Fort Benning Number, October 30, 1940,* Author's collection.)

F.D.R FUNERAL 1945. Roosevelt died April 12, 1945, at his home in Warm Springs. This photo shows Fort Benning soldiers forming an honor guard along the route in downtown Warm Springs as his casket was taken to the train for the trip to Washington during his funeral procession on Friday, April 13. (Courtesy of the National Infantry Museum, gift of Colonel [Ret.] and Mrs. K.B. Blaney.)

PRESIDENT TRUMAN IN 1950. President Harry S Truman arrived on April 21, 1950, to spend the day attending the Joint Orientation Conference. Here he is shown accepting a Follow Me plaque from Infantry School Commandant Maj. Gen. W.A. Burress at a luncheon at the Officers' Club. Truman, in accepting, quipped: "Maybe I'll put it on the back of my train and see if I can get some Republicans." (Courtesy of the National Infantry Museum.)

PRESIDENT JOHNSON IN 1967. President Lyndon Baines Johnson came to Fort Benning on November 10, 1967, for a two-hour visit. He is shown at Doughboy Stadium where he addressed a crowd of 15,000. Maj. Gen. John M. Wright Jr., Infantry School Commandant, is to the left behind Johnson. The visit was part of a whirlwind tour over Veteran's Day weekend to several military installations across the country. (Courtesy of the National Infantry Museum.)

PRESIDENT FORD IN 1975. Gerald Ford spoke in front of the Infantry School on June 14, 1975, to honor the 200th anniversary of the United States Army. Behind Ford, from left to right, are Joe Windsor, Charles S. Daley, James W. Woodruff Jr., of Columbus, all with the Association of the United States Army (AUSA), Georgia governor George D. Busbee, Infantry School Commandant Maj. Gen. Thomas Tarpley, and Howard "Bo" Callaway, Secretary of the Army. (United States Army Photo, courtesy of Gayle Daley Nix.)

GEORGIA'S JIMMY CARTER IN 1978. President Jimmy Carter made no "official" visit to Fort Benning while President. He is shown here on December 26, 1978, at Lawson Field on his return from spending the Christmas holidays in Plains. He and his family greet well-wishers before boarding Air Force One for the return to Washington. (Courtesy of the Jimmy Carter Presidential Library.)

Ten

MEMORIES, MONUMENTS, *and* MOVIES

50TH ANNIVERSARY PARADE, 1968. This parade was held in October 5, 1968, on Broad Street in downtown Columbus to honor the 50th Anniversary of the founding of Fort Benning. Local dignitaries sit in the reviewing stand as the military marches by. A parade with floats followed. (Courtesy of the National Infantry Museum.)

37—Baker Village School, Columbus, Ga.

BAKER HIGH SCHOOL. This high school opened on September 15, 1943, at 1536 Benning Road, off the military base, to serve the children of military families from Fort Benning. It remained a high school until recently, and then became a middle school. The school was named for nearby Baker Village, which was named for Newton D. Baker, Secretary of War from 1916 to 1921. (Curt Teich postcard, Author's collection.)

BAKER VILLAGE/BENNING PARK. This c. 1944 photo shows one of the government housing projects built for Army families. This photograph was taken by Jack Lieberman. (From *The Infantry School, Fort Benning, Georgia* [1944], Author's collection.)

HOWARD BUS LINE. This 1940 advertisement shows the bus service that began in 1921 and by 1941 claimed it had carried millions of passengers from Columbus to Fort Benning and back. The upper photo shows a 1921 bus, the lower one a 1941 model. (From *The Industrial Index, Fort Benning Number, October 30, 1940*, Author's collection.)

AN ENTERTAINMENT SPOT. Many Fort Benning soldiers found entertainment in the clubs and night spots across the Chattahoochee in Phenix City. This club was one of the best known. It went out of business after the massive cleanup of Phenix City that began in 1954. The owner of the club, Mrs. Beachie Howard Parr, known as "Ma Beachie," died in 1983. (From *The Industrial Index, Fort Benning Number, December 5, 1951*, Author's collection.)

PRISONERS OF WAR. During World War II, several thousand German and Italian prisoners of war were brought to Fort Benning. This photo shows Italian POWs in 1943 gathered behind a fence in the Harmony Church area of the base. (From *The Industrial Index, Fort Benning Number, December 29,1943,* courtesy Columbus State University Archives.)

PRISONERS OF WAR. In this photo, the Italian prisoners of war are receiving communion from a priest. Some of the POWs died while prisoners and are buried at the Main Post Cemetery. The POW campsite was on Jamestown Road in the Harmony Church area where a stone and concrete memorial can be found. (From *The Industrial Index, Fort Benning Number, December 29,1943,* courtesy Columbus State University Archives.)

CARRIER PIGEONS. In the 1940s carrier pigeons were raised at Fort Benning and men trained to use them in combat situations. The paratroopers would release them bearing coded messages that the pigeons flew back to notify headquarters of their location after landing behind enemy lines. (From *A Camera Trip* [c.1942], Author's collection.)

SHRINE IN THE WOODS. The Saint Hubert Shrine was built by Private Stadnick near Russ Pond in the 1920s and was restored *c*. 1943. He built it from scraps of tin after his recovery from a serious illness. Photographed in 1944 by Jack Lieberman, the temple was mostly gone by the 1960s. (Courtesy of the Georgia Division of Archives and History and the National Infantry Museum.)

HISTORIC MONUMENT. This monument at the intersection of Lumpkin and Sigerfoos Roads, near the original Bachelor Officer Quarters, was dedicated by the Daughters of the American Revolution and other groups on March 2, 1926, at its original location in the circle in front of the future site of the Infantry School. It was moved here in 1929. Its three bronze plaques honor LaFayette's trip through the region in 1825 (the side seen here), the Federal Road, the Indian village of Kasihta, and the Battle of Hichiti. (Photograph by the author.)

THE CHINESE ARCH. This marble monument photographed *c.* 1944 is located on Morrison Avenue just east of the Officers' Club. It was originally erected in China to honor the 15th Infantry Regiment, part of the international force serving there. On October 13, 1939, after the unit returned stateside, the monument was given to the Infantry School. The inscription was restored in 1983. The photograph was taken by Jack Lieberman. (From *The Infantry School, Fort Benning, Georgia* [1944], Author's collection.)

POW MEMORIAL. Originally dedicated in 1946 at Benning and Cusseta Roads, this monument was moved to Honor Field in 1985; it is in front of the three historic Bachelor Officer Quarters on Richardson Circle. The monument reads: "Dedicated to the Memory of the Men and Women Who Made the Supreme Sacrifice While Prisoners of War In World War II 1941–1945." Additional conflicts and dates covering Korea, Vietnam, and the Middle East have been added. (Photograph by the author.)

WWII RANGER MEMORIAL. This memorial honors the Rangers in World War II and was dedicated on November 14, 1996, by Togo D. West, Secretary of the Army. It is one of many recent monuments erected to honor various Army units at Sacrifice Field, across the road and in front of the National Infantry Museum. (Photograph by the author.)

YOU ARE IN THE MOVIES. Through the years, a number of motion pictures have been made at Fort Benning. This photograph is of the RKO studio team working on the first such movie in 1941, *Parachute Battalion*. The cameraman is identified as Russ Cully, the director with the megaphone is Leslie Goodwins, and the third man is the assistant director, Sammy Ruman. Later movies made at Fort Benning include *Jumping Jacks* (1952), starring Dean Martin and Jerry Lewis; *The Green Berets* (1968), starring John Wayne; *Tank* (1984), starring James Garner and Shirley Jones; *A Time to Triumph* (1986) for TV, starring Patty Duke; *Your Mother Wears Combat Boots* (1989), for TV starring Barbara Eden; and *We Were Soldiers* (2002), starring Mel Gibson. (Courtesy of the Georgia Division of Archives and History and the National Infantry Museum.)

126

BIBLIOGRAPHY

Chronology, 1918–1933.
    Typescript of chronology of Fort Benning's first 15 years. This same chronology was published in *The Columbus Ledger* on October 26, 1933 in the "Fort Benning Anniversary Edition."

Columbus Office Supply Company. *Pictorial Review, Fort Benning, Georgia.* Columbus, GA: Columbus Office Supply Company, *c.* 1943.
    This is the only one of four 1940s picture booklets of Fort Benning with extensive text.

The Doughboy, 1920–1921.
    The annual yearbook of the Infantry School.

Historic Preservation Division, Georgia Department of Natural Resources, Atlanta. National Register of Historic Places and Identified Sites Files for Fort Benning including the Robinson Fisher Associates *Historic Buildings Survey: Fort Benning, Georgia* (1987).

Holcombe, Robert, Jr. *An Outline History of Fort Benning, Georgia and the Infantry School Concept.* Fort Benning: for the National Infantry Museum, 1990. (Unpublished.)

Kane, Sharyn and Richard Keeton. *Fort Benning: The Land and the People.* Fort Benning: United States Army Infantry Center, 1998.
    This is a good look at the prehistoric record of the area and some of the families who lived there prior to the arrival of the United States Army.

Lupold, John S. *Chattahoochee Valley Sources & Resources: An Annotated Bibliography, Volume II: The Georgia Counties.* Eufaula, Alabama: Historic Chattahoochee Commission, 1993.

Muscogiana, the Journal of the Muscogee Genealogical Society. Vol. 6 (3 and 4, Fall 1995)
    Contains several important articles on Fort Benning including a list of people whose property was acquired by the government in 1919–1920s.

National Infantry Museum, Fort Benning. Photograph collection and Fort Benning exhibits.

Reid, Edge, comp. *Ledger References, 1916–1970; Enquirer References, 1950–1970.*
    A valuable index to important local headlines, events, and building news. (Unpublished)

Scipio, L. Albert. *The 24th Infantry at Fort Benning.* Silver Spring, Maryland: Roman Publications, 1986.
    This history of the African-American regiment also includes information on many buildings on post and is a source for many early photographs not included herein.

Telfair, Nancy [Louise Gunby Jones DuBose]. *A History of Columbus, Georgia, 1828–1928.* Columbus: Historical Publishing Company, 1929.
    Contains a good chapter on Fort Benning.

Whitehead, Margaret Laney and Barbara Bogart. *City of Progress: A History of Columbus, Georgia.* Columbus: Columbus Office Supply Company, 1978.

Woodall, W.C. *The Industrial Index.* Magazine published from 1906–1950s. Copies at Columbus State University and the W.C. Bradley Library.

A separate index to its Columbus and Fort Benning photographs exists. The Fort Benning Numbers (annual special editions) for 1940–1943 and 1951 were especially valuable.

Worsley, Etta Blanchard. *Columbus on the Chattahoochee.* Columbus: Columbus Office Supply Company, 1951.

Includes a good history of Fort Benning with many personal anecdotes.

Yarborough, First Lt. Leroy W. and Maj. Truman Smith. *A History of the Infantry School.* Fort Benning: The Infantry School, 1931.

One of several unpublished histories of the school.

INDEX